Published simultaneously in 1995 by Exley Publications in
Great Britain, and Exley Giftbooks in the USA.

12 11 10 9 8 7 6 5 4

ISBN 1-85015-609-3

Edited and pictures selected by Helen Exley.
The moral right of the author has been asserted.
Pictures research by Image Select International.
Typesetting by Delta, Watford.
Printed in China.

Exley Publications Ltd, 16 Chalk Hill, Watford, Herts WD1 4BN, United Kingdom.
Exley Publications LLC, 232 Madison Avenue, Suite 1206, NY 10016, USA.

Acknowledgements: The publishers are grateful for permission to reproduce
copyright material. While every effort has been made to trace copyright holders, the
publishers would be pleased to hear from any not here acknowledged. Leo Buscaglia:
extracts from *Papa, My Father* © Leo F. Buscaglia, Inc., 1989 published by SLACK, Inc.,
New Jersey; Bill Cosby: extract from *Fatherhood*, © William H. Cosby Jr. 1986 published by
Bantam Books, a division of Transworld Publishers, and Bantam, Doubleday, Dell,
Inc.; Berlie Doherty: 'Dad' from *Another First Poetry Book* published by Oxford
University Press 1987; Laurie Lee: extract from *Two Women*, © Laurie Lee 1983, first
published by André Deutsch and by Penguin Books, 1984. Reprinted by permission of
Penguin Books; Ogden Nash: extract from "Soliloquy in Circles" from *Verses from 1929
on*, copyright © 1933, 1948, 1956, renewed 1983 by Ogden Nash. Reprinted by
permission of Curtis Brown Ltd, London and New York, and by Little Brown &
Company, Boston.
Picture Credits: Exley Publications is very grateful to the following individuals and
organizations for permission to reproduce their pictures: Alinari (ALI), Archiv für
Kunst (AKG), Art Resource (AR), Bridgeman Art Library (BAL), Christie's Colour
Library (CCL), Fine Art Photographic Library (FAP), Giraudon (GIR), Scala (SCA).
Cover: Henri-Francois Riesener (GIR); title page: Henry Scott Tuke (CCL); page 7:
Arthur Hacker (BAL); page 8/9: D. Ghirlandaio (AR/SCA); page 10: Bartolomene
Esteban Murillo (AKG); page 13: Sir Lawrence Alma-Tadema (EDM); page 15: Bernard
de Hoog (CCL); page 17: Giuseppe Moricci, SCA); page 19: Francesco Gimeno (Index/
BAL); page 20/21: P. Nomellini (ALI); page 22/23: Carl Spitzweig (AKG); page 24:
©1995 William H. Johnson, untitled, National Museum of American Art (BAL); page
27: P. Bortnov (EDM); page 28: Albert Neuhuys (CCL); page 31: Veronese (SCA); page
33: Federico Zandomeneghi (SCA); page 35: P. Nomellini (ALI); page 37: Alvar Jansson,
Statens Konstmuseer, Stockholm; page 39: Edgar Degas (AKG); page 40: ©1995 G.
Bondzin, "Annemone" (AKG); page 42: Emilie Mundi (EDM); page 45: Mario Marcucci
(SCA); page 46: T. Gaponenko (EDM); page 48/49: ©1995 Willi Balendat, "Watching the
Fair" (AKG); page 50/51: V. A. Arlashin, Roy Miles Gallery (BAL); page 53: Henri
Manguin (AR); page 54: M. Trufanov (EDM); page 56: G. Ciardi (SCA); page 59: ©1995
Edward Weiss "Billy Rose", National Museum of American Art (AR); page 60/61: P.
Nomellini (ALI).

If God brings you to it,
He will bring you through it,

FROM MOTHER EDNA

THE BEST OF

FATHER

QUOTATIONS

A HELEN EXLEY GIFTBOOK

Be the Keeper of the FAMILY TREASURES

EXLEY
NEW YORK • WATFORD, UK

THE SPIRIT OF LOVE

"A man prides himself on his strength –
but when his child is born
discovers overnight that strength is
not enough, and that he must
learn gentleness."

PAM BROWN, b.1928

"Wife, the Athenians rule the Greeks,
and I rule the Athenians, and thou me,
and our son thee; let him then use
sparingly the authority which makes
him, foolish as he is, the most powerful
person in Greece."

THEMISTOCLES (c.523 - c.458 B.C.)

"She climbed into my lap and curled into
the crook of my left arm. I couldn't move
that arm, but I could cradle Ashtin in it. I
could kiss the top of her head. And I could
have no doubt that this was one of the
sweetest moments in my life."

DENNIS BYRD,
about his daughter

"No man can possibly know what life means, what the world means, what anything means, until he has a child and loves it.

And then the whole universe changes and nothing will ever again seem exactly as it seemed before."

LAFCADIO HEARN (1850 - 1904)

"When a father sets out to teach his little son to walk, he stands in front of him and holds his two hands on either side of the child, so that he cannot fall, and the boy goes toward his father between his father's hands. But the moment he is close to his father, he moves away a little and holds his hands farther apart, and he does this over and over, so that the child may learn to walk."

THE BAAL SHEM

"And who was I to her? The rough dark shadow of pummelling games and shouts, the cosy frightener, the tossing and swinging arms, lifting the body to the highest point of hysteria before lowering it back again to the safe male smell.
But she was my girl now, the second force in my life, and with her puffed, knowing eyes, forever moving with colour and light, she was well aware of it."

LAURIE LEE, b.1914,
from "Two Women"

"It is the family's expectation that will make father into his best and biggest self."

SAMUEL S. DRURY,
from "Fathers & Sons"

"There is no other success for a father and a mother except to feel that they have made some contribution to the development of their children."

JOSEPH P. KENNEDY (1888 - 1969)

"No one knows the true worth of a man but his family. The dreary man drowsing, drop-jawed, in the commuter train, the office bore, the taciturn associate – may be the pivot of a family's life, welcomed with hugs, told the day's news, asked for advice. No longer Mr. B, but Dad. No longer a nonentity but a man possessed of skills and wisdom; courageous and capable, patient and kind. Respected and loved."

PAM BROWN, b.1928

"I might have a sex change operation and become a nun, but outside of that I do not think my life could possibly have changed more than it did by becoming a father. And when my son looks up at me and breaks into his wonderful toothless smile, my eyes fill up and I know that having him is the best thing I will ever do."

DAN GREENBERG

"Last night my child was born.... If you ever become a father, I think the strangest and strongest sensation of your life will be hearing for the first time the thin cry of your own child. For a moment you have the strange feeling of being double; but there is something more, quite impossible to analyze – perhaps the echo in a man's heart of all the sensations felt by all fathers and mothers at a similar instant in the past. It is a very tender, but also a very ghostly feeling."

LAFCADIO HEARN (1850 - 1904),
from his "Letters"

"Safe, for a child, is his father's hand,
holding him tight."
MARION C. GARRETTY, b.1917

"Across his front was a gold watch chain
with a big tick-tock watch on the end. In
my own children's time it also had a
chocolate tree which flowered into silver-
paper-covered chocolates.
All about him was safe."
NAOMI MITCHISON, b.1897

"I could not point to any need in
childhood as strong as that for a
father's protection."
SIGMUND FREUD (1856 - 1939)

"A dad is a man haunted by death, fears,
anxieties. But who seems to his children
the haven from all harm. And who makes
them certain that whatever happens – it
will all come right."
CLARA ORTEGA, b.1955

INVITO
ALLA FORMAZIONE
DELLE SOCIETÀ
DI MUTUO SOCCORSO
PER LE ARTI E MESTIERI
ITALIA 1851

"Fatherhood, for me, has been less a job than an unstable and surprising combination of adventure, blindman's bluff, guerrilla warfare and crossword puzzle."

FREDERIC F. VAN DE WATER,
from "Fathers are Funny"

"We start out imitating the heroes – Bogart, Cagney, Eastwood, the outlaws and rogues who make their own rules. Then along come the children and nothing is ever the same. Suddenly Mr. I'll-Handle-This is wearing a Flintstones cap and reaching under the couch for some stray peas. Suddenly the man who would be the Duke has oatmeal on his shoes."

HUGH O'NEILL

"A child enters your home and for the next twenty years makes so much noise you can hardly stand it. The child departs, leaving the house so silent you think you are going mad."

JOHN ANDREW HOLMES

"The words that a father speaks
to his children in the privacy of
home are not heard by the world,
but, as in whispering-galleries,
they are clearly heard at the end and
by posterity."

JEAN PAUL RICHTER (1763 - 1825)

"Words have an awesome impact. The impressions made by a father's voice can set in motion an entire trend of life."

GORDON MacDONALD

"There are no stories quite like the very first Dad stories."

H. DALTON, b.1966

"You can learn many things from children.
How much patience you have,
for instance."

FRANKLIN P. JONES

"There are times when parenthood
seems nothing but feeding the mouth
that bites you."
PETER DE VRIES

"Dads are stone skimmers, mud wallowers, water wallopers, ceiling swoopers, shoulder gallopers, upsy-downsy, over-and-through, round-and-about whooshers. Dads are smugglers and secret sharers."

HELEN THOMSON, b.1943

"To show a child what has once delighted you, to find the child's delight added to your own so that there is now a double delight seen in the glow of trust and affection, this is happiness."

J.B. PRIESTLEY (1894 - 1984)

DAD

Dad is the dancing-man
The laughing-bear, the prickle-chin,
The tickle-fingers, jungle-roars,
Bucking bronco, rocking-horse,
The helicopter roundabout
The beat-the-wind at swing-and-shout
Goal-post, scarey-ghost,
Climbing-Jack, humpty-back.

But sometimes he's
A go-away-please!
A snorey-snarl, a sprawly slump
A yawny mouth, a sleepy lump,

And I'm a kite without a string
Waiting for Dad to dance again.

BERLIE DOHERTY

"One moment's obedience to natural law and an ordinary man finds himself called upon to be wise, kindly, patient, loving, dispenser of justice, arbiter of truth, consultant paediatrician, expert in education, financial wizard, mender of toys, source of all knowledge, master of skills.

And to wake one day to find that he has failed and that he is, after all, a silly old devil who's out of touch and out of date. He should not be discouraged. He will eventually be reinstated."

PETER GRAY, b.1928

"The chances are that you will never be elected president of the country, write the great American novel, make a million dollars, stop pollution, end racial conflict, or save the world. However valid it may be to work at any of these goals, there is another one of higher priority – to be an effective parent."

LANDRUM R. BOLLING

"Of all nature's gifts to the human race, what is sweeter to a man than his children?"

CICERO (106 - 43 B.C.)

"Arthur always had his arms around [his daughter] Camera. When he talked about her, his face would light up like stars in the sky. He showed more feeling for his daughter than I had seen him show his whole life."

HORACE ASHE,
uncle of Arthur Ashe

But after you've raised them
and educated and gowned them,
They just take their little fingers
and wrap you around them.

Being a father
Is quite a bother,
But I like it, rather.

OGDEN NASH (1902 - 1971)
from "Soliloquy In Circles"

"First and foremost, they are our fathers;
and whatever magic we had with them,
even if for just a few of our very early
years, profoundly affects us for the rest
of our lives."

CYRA McFADDEN

"She didn't love her father – she *idolized*
him. He was the one great love in her life.
No other man ever measured up to him."

MARY S. LOVELL,
about Beryl Markham

"Dad is proud of the buildings he's put up
over the years. To me, none of these can
match the little things he made just for me
with his two hands."

SUZANNE CHAZIN

"Directly after God in heaven
comes Papa."

WOLFGANG AMADEUS MOZART (1756 - 1791)

"How sad that men would base an entire civilization on the principle of paternity, upon the legal ownership and presumed responsibility for children, and then never get to know their sons and daughters very well."

PHYLLIS CHESLER

"The father who holds the baby only when it is sweet and fresh; who plays on the nursery floor when things go along like a song; who gingerly tiptoes away at times of tears or disciplinary show-downs, is just a dilettante papa, with a touch of the coward, and not a complete father."

SAMUEL S. DRURY,
from "Fathers & Sons"

"He who brings up, not he who begets, is the father."

EXODUS 34:3

"It is easier for a father to have children than for children to have a real father."

POPE JOHN XXIII (1881 - 1963)

"I talk and talk and talk, and I haven't taught people in fifty years what my fathe taught by example in one week."

MARIO CUOMO

"One father is more than a hundred schoolmasters."

GEORGE HERBERT (1593 - 1633)

"By looking at us, listening to us, hearing us, respecting our opinions, affirming our value, giving us a sense of dignity, he was unquestionably our most influential teacher."

LEO BUSCAGLIA,
from "Papa, My Father"

"A wise father teaches skills. Courage. Concentration on the job in hand. Self discipline. Encourages enthusiasm. A spirit of enquiry. Gentleness. Kindliness. Patience. Courtesy. And Love."

PAM BROWN, b.1928

"Wallace Stevens defined a poet as a 'connoisseur of chaos,' which is a perfect way for any daddy who would survive the darkest hours to think of himself. You've got to love the madness. 'With a great poet,' wrote Keats, 'the sensing of Beauty overcomes every consideration.' Amid the storm, there is only the color of your son's hair."

HUGH O'NEILL

"Children are a great comfort in your old age – and they help you reach it faster, too."

LIONEL KAUFMAN

"Performance under stress is one test of effective leadership. It may also be the proof of accomplishment when it comes to evaluating the quality of a father."

GORDON MacDONALD

"Insanity is hereditary; you can get it from your children."

SAM LEVENSON

"Parents are sometimes a bit of a
disappointment to their children.
They don't fulfil the promise of their
early years."

ANTHONY POWELL, b.1905

"Dads show off.
Sadly, dads also fall off, through
and under."

PETER GRAY, b.1928

"Unless he happens to work for Halston,
the American father cannot be trusted to
put together combinations of clothes. He is
a man who was taught that the height of
fashion was to wear two shoes that
matched; and so, children can easily
convince him of the elegance of whatever
they do or don't want to wear."

BILL COSBY, b.1937

"Children are unpredictable. You never
know what inconsistency they're going to
catch you in next."

FRANKLIN P. JONES

"The secret of dealing successfully with a child is not to be its parent."
MELL LAZARUS ·

"There are three ways to get something done: do it yourself, hire someone, or forbid your kids to do it."
MONTA CRANE

"Reasoning with a child is fine, if you can reach the child's reason without destroying your own."
JOHN MASON BROWN

"Heredity is what a man believes in until his son begins to behave like a delinquent."
from "Presbyterian Life"

"Get even. Live long enough to be a problem to your kids."
ANONYMOUS

"Parents are the bones on which children
sharpen their teeth."
PETER USTINOV, b.1921

"In every dispute between parent and
child, both cannot be right, but
they may be, and usually are, both
wrong. It is this situation which
gives family life its peculiar
hysterical charm."
ISAAC ROSENFELD

"If you have never been hated by your
child, you have never been a parent."
BETTE DAVIS (1908 - 1989)

"When I was a boy of fourteen, my father
was so ignorant I could hardly stand to
have the old man around. But when I got
to be twenty-one, I was astounded at
how much the old man had learned
in seven years."
MARK TWAIN (1835 - 1910)

"On Open Days teachers are inclined to greet dads with a certain cynicism. They've marked the homework."

MAYA V. PATEL, b.1943

"As we read the school reports upon our children, we realize with a sense of relief that can rise to delight that thank Heavens – nobody is reporting in this fashion upon us."

J.B. PRIESTLEY (1894 - 1984)

"There comes a time when you have to face the fact that Dad has forgotten how to do algebra."

CHARLOTTE GRAY, b.1937

"A father is...
...an ordinary man
doing his best to stand in for Superman.
...a source of good but usually
expendable advice.
...a very-nearly expert.
...a man who knows – but would like to
look it up just to be on the safe side.
...a man who goes down fighting."

PAM BROWN, b.1928

"...my father would pick me up and
hold me high in the air.
He dominated my life as long as he lived,
and was the love of my life for many
years after he died."

ELEANOR ROOSEVELT (1884 - 1962)

"I was my father's daughter.... He is dead
now and I am a grown woman and still I
am my father's daughter.... I am many
things besides, but I am daddy's girl too
and so I will remain – all the way to the
old folks' home."

PAULA WEIDEGER

"I was not close to my father, but he
was very special to me.
Whenever I did something as a little girl –
learn to swim or act in a school play, for
instance – he was fabulous. There would
be this certain look in his eyes.
It made me feel great."

DIANE KEATON

A little child, a limber elf singing,
dancing to itself.... Make such a vision to
the sight, as fills a father's eyes with light.
SAMUEL TAYLOR COLERIDGE (1772 - 1834)

"Children are poor men's riches."
THOMAS FULLER (1608 - 1661)

"Dad, when you come home at night with only shattered pieces of your dreams, your little one can mend them like new with two magic words – 'Hi Dad!'."
ALAN BECK

"Literature is mostly about having sex and not much about having children. Life is the other way around."
DAVID DODGE

"The child you want to raise as an upright
and honorable person requires a lot more
of your time than your money."
GEORGE VARKY

"There has been a succession of women's revolutions.... But watch out for the revolt of the father, if he should get fed up with feeding others, and get bored with being used, and lay down his tools, and walk off to consult his soul."

MAX LERNER

"Fathers went hunting and left their wives to guard the cave.
Fathers went off to war and left the village to their dames.
Fathers sailed over the horizon and left their womenfolk to work and weep.
Let's start again.
Fathers hold their babies close.
Fathers and mothers share the commonplace.
And the adventure.
Fatherhood is discovering that life outweighs flamboyant death.
And kind companionship outlasts possession."

PAM BROWN, b.1928

"Parenthood isn't a picnic. Dad may work from sun to sun, but as a father he's never done."

WILLIAM D. WILKINS

"I watched a small man with thick calluses on both hands work fifteen and sixteen hours a day.
I saw him once literally bleed from the bottoms of his feet, a man who came here uneducated, alone, unable to speak the language, who taught me all I needed to know about faith and hard work by the simple eloquence of his example."

MARIO CUOMO

"I feel perhaps that you do not think I appreciate the single-heartedness of your life, your sturdy unselfishness and the sacrifice of ambition for the sake of your family."

SIR COMPTON MacKENZIE (1883 - 1972),
to his father

"Papa never climbed Everest or made the 'Guinness Book of World Records'. He never read the classics or saw an original painting by Braque. He never played baseball and rarely won at bocce ball. He was born poor and, in spite of his working hard all his life, he was always poor. He was proud, self-taught, and left no debts. If he had any hidden dreams, other than of being a good man, a committed father, and a loving husband, no one ever knew about them. If deep regrets, fears, or personal doubts tormented him, he never stated them.

I am aware that years of having known and loved my father have transformed him from Papa, the simple human being, into Papa, the near saint. And I've come to the conclusion that there is nothing wrong with that."

LEO BUSCAGLIA,
from "Papa, My Father"

"Your hands have changed with the years – grown a little out of shape and worn. But for me they are the hands that held me steady on your shoulders, that taught me sailors' knots, that soothed away my nightmare, that kept me safe. Any change in them is only a disguise. They are the hands I trust, the hands that now, as then, mean certainty and love."

PAM BROWN, b.1928

"One day, when the children are grown, dads mean to drop the mask and take up where they left off. It comes as a shock to discover they have lost twenty years or so – and that they are balding. And the children tower above them, and pat them on the head."

CLARA ORTEGA, b.1955

"We do not care how many wrinkles he may have or how his rheumatism makes him limp or how the gray colors his hair, he is still the same great man and the object of our love and adoration."

LEROY BROWNLOW,
from "A Father's World"

"Dads don't need to be tall and broad-shouldered and handsome and clever. Love makes them so."

PAM BROWN, b.1928

"I know fame and power are for the birds. But then suddenly life comes into focus for me. And, ah, there stand my kids. I love them."

LEE IACOCCA, b.1924